# The Day Clocks Spoke Russian

André de Korvin

Transcendent Zero Press
Houston, Texas

Copyright © 2016, André de Korvin.

PUBLISHED BY TRANSCENDENT ZERO PRESS
www.transcendentzeropress.org

All rights reserved. No part or parts of this book may be reproduced in any format, except for portions used in reviews, without the expressed written consent from the author or from the publisher.

ISBN-13: 978-0692640081

ISBN-10: 0692640088

Printed in the United States of America

Library of Congress Control Number: 2016933024

Cover design by Glynn Monroe Irby
Cover photo image of Earl Irby

FIRST EDITION
Transcendent Zero Press

# The Day Clocks Spoke Russian

André de Korvin

**I dedicate this book of poems
to my wonderful parents**

*Nina and Vladimir Korvin-Piotrowsky*

# Introduction

I am writing this introduction on an evening following Great Britain's recent withdrawal from the European Union, what we now call Brexit, and in this moment of economic tumult, I recognize even more fully the wisdom of the poems which comprise André de Korvin's *The Day Clocks Spoke Russian*. He writes in the volume's preface, "The world grew older. Stocks went up and down like heartbeats of a terminally ill patient." And this patient is the world and those heartbeats, the pulse of global capitalism in decline. De Korvin's poems emerge out of his visceral knowledge of having lived through the latter half of the 20th and early 21st centuries as an émigré born in Berlin to Russian parents, subsequently raised in Paris, and finally coming to live in the United States, first in Los Angeles and later in Houston.

> The color of my country was
> part fog and part blood.
> I still remember the language
> the water spoke…
>
> ["Many Years Ago"]

The poems are informed by de Korvin's keen sense of European history, both east and west, and his understanding of the socioeconomic forces shaping our daily lives. This collection is the story of a life—his own, the reader's—understood as the uncertain intersection of individual erotic imagination and political history. The volume begins with the poet's own conception in the poem "Intersection," when he writes of his parents, Nina and Vladimir Korvin-Piotrowsky, to whom the book is dedicated:

> She left St. Petersburg
> when she was fifteen.
> Her parents bought her
> a one way ticket to Berlin.
> He drifted from Kiev
> through the fields of Poland,
> Cyrillic letters raining
> where he went.
> They sat in a small library
> where poetry stretched
> wide on the shelves…

It's important to know that de Korvin's father, Vladimir, was a significant Russian poet whose own poems have helped to shape his son's life and work. One evening at his townhome, de Korvin played for my husband and me a recording of his father performing his poems in Russian, and though I could not understand the words, I recall distinctly their ringing, incantatory power, one marking his son's lifelong engagement with verse.

> I was already there,
> a small spark flaring
> in the dark
> above their beds.
>
> ["Intersection"]

I first came to know André de Korvin as mathematician not poet. He was a faculty colleague at the University of Houston-Downtown where for more than twenty years he served as professor of computer and applied mathematical sciences. He has particular expertise in the mathematical theory of evidence, uncertainty in expert systems, knowledge acquisition, and fuzzy logic—an approach to computation that is based on "degrees of truth" rather a presumed certainty, and he has published more than 200 scholarly articles on these topics. But for me, what is most compelling about de Korvin's career in the sciences is the intersection of that computational work with poetry, where fuzzy logic mirrors the dream logic of metaphor, where the precision of clockworks becomes the uncertainty of human history, of our understanding of time itself. I first read de Korvin's poems as part of his second book, *Dreaming Indigo Time* published in 2005, and some of the same themes infusing those poems are present in this volume. De Korvin is concerned with time and the ways in which scientists and philosophers have interrogated it—whether Newton or Einstein or Heidegger. He sees time, perhaps as Heidegger does, as an enveloping present where past and future exist simultaneously in our conscious experience of the present moment—as both memory and anticipation of what is to come. The book's inaugural poem is called "Time Travel," and two poems later, in "There Were Rumors," he writes:

> History had derailed,
> a runaway train causing the future
> to wrap itself around the past.
> The reason, some said, was time fatigue…
> clouds were losing blood
> drifting East like wounded horses
> and the sun rolling across cities was
> the dial of a broken clock showing
> two minutes to disaster.

Economics too is a critical theme in these poems, where money, "the pale ghost rising…lit everything, green flames/on the snow white lips of marble statues," where the course of human history is shaped by greed. He writes, "Fed by world-wide rumors/$$$ signs flew/on the flags of all nations" ["Rumors of Money"] or "Poverty smiles,/her language is not pretty/when she stumbles/through the census bureau,/ messing up the GNP" ["The Priest Next Door"].

De Korvin engages the vocabularies of multiple social systems—political, philosophical, economic, scientific, technological, artistic—to position his verse beyond the confessional within a larger cultural and historical frame. More than the simple tracing de Korvin's life from Paris to the United States, we see in the book's architecture a mythic trajectory—six carefully crafted sections that trace the cycles of a human life. De Korvin posits that we begin in "Rumors," that slice of time, before we are born, that later belongs to us—the immediate past we discover through the accounts of others. We move then to childhood with its baffling ironies, to adolescent violence, sexual exploits and concomitant self-interrogation, to adulthood, the alienation of middle age, and beyond to the losses that accumulate with aging.

This cycle too can be seen historically in de Korvin's use of sardonic wit in the service of cultural critique as he depicts for the reader the brutally dispiriting era in which his own life emerged. The poems' trajectory also trace the lives of all those whose personal history has been intertwined with that of 20th-century Europe, Great Britain, and the United States—from the rise of World War II and the atrocities of mass murders, to the totalitarianism of the Soviet era and the Cold War, to the fall of communism in 1989, and the subsequent advance of global capitalism as the new colonialism. From such lines as "countries expanded and contracted/like rubber balls about to tear" ["When The Curtain Moved"] to "Mirages invade the city,/evening sees the whole sky/burning…" ["Nocturnal Citizenship"], we too experience the unpredictability of history's course. We may acknowledge the inevitability of error, greed, the illusory nature of our perceptions as human beings over time. And yet we continue, we look back, look forward, anticipate the possibilities of each new era—as the poet shows us in his closing poem: "Coming out of the subway," the subterranean of the poetic imagination, into sunlight on wet pavement, so that "Dust start[s] to sing again…/rain curling gently/poems around [our] fingers"["There Came A Time"].

What happens, then, when a mechanical timepiece begins to speak in a language other than mathematics? What happens when that language is one tied both to 20th-century European history, economics, the lifespan of global capitalism—and simultaneously to the mother/father tongue, the language of poetry? What we discover is that these poems are also about home, what we hold sacred in the face of uncertainty. The beloved connections we weave, carry with us, day to day, country to country, language to language, as our interior lives. These poems address aging, death, the inevitability of loss, so that our lives become a "River Café" of what flows before us, past us, leaving us bereft. But they also craft light, a steadfast place for love, the consolation of its redemptive power.

> Those who recognize light
> for what it really is,
> an endless garden where
> music lives its second life,
> they will hear night sing
> departure to every dawn.

["What The Gypsy Told Me"]

It is in this intersection of the poet's deeply personal encounter with his humanity, with history and the languages—Russian, French, English—he carries, crafts, that we discover the genius of André de Korvin's poetry, and the clocks begin to speak for us as well.

Robin Davidson,<br>
City of Houston Poet Laureate<br>
June 29, 2016

# Table of Contents

**Introduction by Robin Davidson**..................................*vii-xiii*

**I Rumors**......................................................................**19**
    Time Travel...............................................................*21*
    Intersection..............................................................*22*
    There Were Rumors................................................*23*
    Rumors Of Money...................................................*24*
    Rumors Of Glory.....................................................*25*
    Hunger......................................................................*26*
    I Died Young............................................................*27*
    Many Years Ago......................................................*28*
    When The Curtain Moved.....................................*29*
    Exit............................................................................*30*

**II We Wept Icons On Parisian Cobblestones**..........**31**
    Arrival.......................................................................*33*
    Reading Music Leaves............................................*34*
    The Fall.....................................................................*35*
    I Remember.............................................................*36*
    First Conversations.................................................*37*
    A Shooting Star.......................................................*38*
    French Lessons........................................................*39*
    To Mr. Vanee...........................................................*40*
    Blue Horizons..........................................................*41*
    It Was A Time..........................................................*42*

**III The Lessons Of The Glass**......................................**43**
    At night.....................................................................*45*

Warriors.................................................................. *46*

Way To Go............................................................. *47*

The Music Lesson.................................................. *48*

Let The Good Times Roll....................................... *49*

Children's Park...................................................... *50*

Through The Glass, Darkly.................................... *51*

My Lamp................................................................ *52*

Ma Bell.................................................................. *53*

The Season Of Changes........................................ *54*

**IV Mr. Bureaucracy, Sister Alienation............... 55**

The Passport......................................................... *57*

Eclipse.................................................................. *58*

Sister Alienation................................................... *59*

Bad Neighborhood................................................ *60*

Mr. Bureaucracy Moved In.................................... *61*

Nocturnal Citizenship........................................... *62*

What The Gypsy Told Me...................................... *63*

Painting Time....................................................... *64*

They Scream *Jordan*........................................... *65*

The Priest Next Door............................................ *66*

**V River Café.......................................................... 67**

It's Not Easy......................................................... *69*

Color Blue............................................................ *70*

Later In Life......................................................... *71*

Clockwork Winding Down..................................... *72*

Disease................................................................ *73*

Once Upon A Time............................................... *74*

When I Sleep....................................................... *75*

| | |
|---|---|
| The Visitor | *76* |
| Regrets | *77* |
| At The River Café | *78* |
| **VI Riding The Subway** | ***79*** |
| Reasons | *81* |
| You're Gone | *82* |
| Coming Home | *83* |
| Long Distance | *84* |
| Conversations | *85* |
| Intersection II | *86* |
| Jim And I | *87* |
| End Of A Republic | *88* |
| Memory | *89* |
| There Came A Time | *90* |

*Rumors were starting to drown daily conversations. Reports came from cities and villages that clocks tried to speak Russian. There were stories of errors that would lead to global disasters. Clocks were beginning to speak of hunger stalking children, of armies massing at border towns, of money burning, burning...*

*Soon after, we took to the streets and wept icons on the hard pavements of Europe. Bad music played death, played blood. Objects, ideas and dead people came alive. Grammar came too, limping across Cyrillic stanzas. Some of us carried winter inside our bodies, some grew wings. Many took passports and immigrated to other worlds...*

*Broken glass littered the streets, accurately reflecting a shattered world. Earth went on turning with its great seas of blood. Mr. Bureaucracy and sister Alienation followed us. We walked through lethal neighborhoods. Clocks spoke razor blades, spoke wounded horses. My eyelids became butterflies and soared over a half written poem about war. Mr. Bureaucracy tried, unsuccessfully, to silence clocks...*

*The world grew older. Stocks went up and down like heartbeats of a terminally ill patient. We took the subway and although we ended up on the dark side of time, the profound voices of these clocks kept telling us we could still take other roads that would not lead us to the dark of time.*

# I Rumors

## Time Travel

When you sleep
in your star-shaped room
and clocks stand by your bed
marking time like
widows that remember
and defunct images sink
deeper into the paleness
trailing an eraser's path,
that's when the ceiling
leans toward you
its white surface sad
and paler than a geisha's face.
Cloud by cloud
you assemble the sky
waiting for it
to open like a curtain
to the drama of your life.
When the dead speak
you watch absence
soaring  gently
from the stanzas of your draft.

## Intersection

She left St. Petersburg
when she was fifteen.
Her parents bought her
a one way ticket to Berlin.
He drifted from Kiev
through the fields of Poland,
Cyrillic letters raining
where he went.
They sat in a small library
where poetry stretched
wide on the shelves,
wider than politics,
wider than philosophy,
wider than physics and
I was already there,
a small spark flaring
in the dark
above their beds.

## There Were Rumors

Some monumental error had occurred.
History had derailed,
a runaway train causing the future
to wrap itself around the past.
The reason, some said, was time fatigue.
There were rumors
sunsets were not really taking place,
clouds were losing blood
drifting East like wounded horses
and the sun rolling across cities was
the dial of a broken clock showing
two minutes to disaster.

## Rumors Of Money

They all dreamed
themselves smiling
on bills of high denomination,
a soaring eagle or a palace
in the back of their heads.
Fed by world-wide rumors
$$$ sign flew
on the flags of all nations.
Statues of defunct heroes stood,
arms wide open, as if praying
for a vaster world. At funerals,
Money was the pale ghost rising
from the mouths of dead merchants
and at night in churches
it lit everything, green flames
on the snow white lips
of marble saints

## Rumors Of Glory

There were rumors of armies
pushing buttons all summer long,
of guns twisting like snakes
to fire at friendly troops,
of war with a shovel in its bloody hands
singing the national anthem
as it buried the dead,
of Glory turning into a whore,
sleeping around with admirals,
Glory too busy to attend
funerals of unknown soldiers.

## Poverty

moved in with its truck
loads of sleepless hours.
It went to bed with many children.
They said economy was real depressed.
Bureaucrats blamed telephone poles
for staring at the moon,
blamed the moon for being tardy,
blamed time for reckless speeding.
From tall buildings you saw people
lying prone in parking lots
and you imagined their deaths
as pale stars falling on the black
asphalt of poor neighborhoods
and you saw their bodies as footnotes,
as asterisk markers, as lights fading
and indifference pacing
the longest street of the world.

# I Died Young

I sit on the hill, motionless.
Rain comes after the sun,
snow comes after the rain.
Green leaves turn yellow
then red and fall.
They took down the school,
built a shopping mall.
The village grows into a town,
the town into a city.
I sit on the hill motionless,
waiting for resurrection.

I'm the poem that started
with a beautiful promise.
I was young, often running
with the wrong crowd,
inhaling what New York
literary gangsters were saying.
I wanted life to sing loud
and clear through my verses.
They machine gunned
every line that tried
to sing it like it was.
My images now
all cinders and ashes.

## Many Years Ago

I forgot the river's name
because I was far from home.
Thereafter, I called it Autumn River,
although I don't think
it was the right name.
The color of my country was
part fog and part blood.
I still remember the language
the water spoke and that's why
I remain an émigré
unable to unlearn
my foreign way of speaking.

## When The Curtain Moved

The world had already
gotten smaller
and countries expanded and
contracted
like rubber balls about to tear.
The hospital clock had a missing hand,
so its ticking rose and fell like
heartbeats of a terminally ill patient.
My father slowly walked
into the waiting room,
blew smoke circles
over the lampshade and said:
*Last night I dreamed*
*Tchaikovsky standing*
*silent on our street,*
*one of his wings was broken.*
*Seven musicians were leaning*
*hands raised against the wall.*
*I think war will start*
*in a couple of days.*

## Exit

In this landscape, I said
grammar is blood
and heartbeats
the spoken words.
In this landscape, pulses
running through your body
are punctuation marking
the depth of each sentence.
Beyond, there's the blinding light,
500 watts carelessly tossed
all over the surgery room.
There's the man who will cut
you with his knife and the clerk
who will write your name.
On a long white table,
in between contractions,
my mother imagines me
coming into this world.
My first scream rises
from the depth of her dream,
an echo caught somewhere
between dark waters
and white clouds.

# II  We Wept Icons

# On Parisian Cobblestones

# Arrival

War rode into town
in its red wagon,
with its fake jewelry,
its anthems tumbling from bullhorns,
its generals sporting rainbow stripes
on their grasshopper color coats,
its drill sergeants heading the parade,
*left right left right kill*
*Left right left right*
*you know we will,*
its cheap wrong-year calendars,
its watches running against time,
its crystal balls predicting
a bright future and
hard days ahead,
its politicians hustling,
hiding casualties in their sleeves,
making death disappear,
always talking numbers,
always talking money and
never never revealing
the true cost of war.

## Reading Music Leaves

Bad music stood up
and started walking,
stumbling like a drunken sailor.
These weren't the beautiful songs
written by people who thought
pianos had wings,
this was guts and guns music.
It was bound to explode
like oranges thrown
by angry policemen
at poets signing
iambic peace petitions.
Those oranges were red
so some warned
there would be blood
wherever you stood.

## The Fall

When I fell for the first time,
I thought ducks and squirrels would call
my guardian angel on the phone
and trees would grow hands
just to hold me up.
Stones refused to roll away, flowers
didn't want to blossom into pillows.
When I fell, pain came running,
its feet hardly touching ground.
It held me in its arms
for the longest time.

# I Remember

Miriam on her bed, drifting away
on strong currents of hallucinations
and Scarlet Fever pacing,
unwanted guest in her small room.
I remember we lost our way
to the funeral home.
The sun was sinking low.
Death wearing dark glasses
went by, talking to itself
about fated failures
and crazy resurrections.
I remember we kept circling
Anger Drive, it was
a one way street.
A little girl who was
Miriam's friend said:
*Miriam better not go up there*
*because the sky has fever*
*look, the sky's all red.*

## First Conversations

I asked the Russian priest
Which way to dark river?
Being one year old,
I didn't speak very well
the language of my parents,
also my voice came out
somewhat distorted
by the émigré sadness
I carried within.
It sounded like this:
ma-ma- ma-ma.
The priest, he got very angry
his words came at me
like an engine
that was losing steam:
hush-hush-hush-hush.
I still remember
the kitchen curtains waving
in the summer wind,
Earth's gentle sway,
the Russian priest
and all of us
falling through the stars.

# A Shooting Star

One day Napoleon departed
from all my history books.
His new empire became
my long poem in progress.
He loved to beat up bullies,
waiting for action
in empty streets
outside school.
His face was white as ice,
so in time he became
smaller
on account of the heat
generated by his heart.
He didn't know back then
he would be killed
by a shooting star
that one day came
crashing down, totally destroying
stanza twelve and
badly maiming thirteen
in that long and pointless poem
that started with half truths
and ended with half war.

## French Lessons

Grammar came to our lessons,
a mean old witch waving compositions
as if they were flags of alien lands.
Names went up, bleak barricades
across fields of wild growing verbs.
She fired endless rounds of
clauses, phrases and morphemes
at the music of children
speaking foreign tongues,
so they stopped sensing rhythm
the same way we ignore the sky
when we look up to watch
the crane slowly swinging
its rusted wrecking ball.

## To Mr. Vanee

Children who had imagination said:
Mr. Vanee, our math teacher,
is made of empty space.
I can still see him ascending
the steps of our school,
apathy on his heels
like a dog on a leash.
Years later, he's a corpse
in all of my rough drafts,
his grave marked
by crossed off stanzas,
and the whiteness of the page
blazes like the winter
he carried within.

## Blue Horizons

Men in green surrounded him.
Cars slowly came to a stop,
a clockwork ready to wind down.
His face was whiter than the door
with the no exit sign
he kept seeing in his dream,
white as bones
in black parking lots.
Every window reflected
the four clouds that were
just hanging there.
He thought: *in two seconds*
*bullets will fly*
*like exclamation points*
*to punctuate the end of my life!!!*
The sun went darker than official
stamps on his foreign passport
and suddenly airborne
he grew wings,
one more immigrant
on the vertical road
to blue horizons.

## It Was A Time

Prince Obolensky
went into exile and fountains
in Luxembourg Gardens
refused to weep Cyrillic letters.
It was a time
loneliness rose
late at night
to her second floor apartment,
broken wing
trailing on the steps.
It was a time
my father stood
at the doors of the Russian church,
icons tumbling from his eyes
on Parisian cobblestones.

# III The Lessons Of The Glass

## At night

I would walk
streets with foreign names:
Rue des Innocents,
Rue du Cochon qui sommeille,
Rue de la Decharge.
For hours, I would watch
trucks and listen
as they went over bridges
like bows
across violin strings.

# Warriors

We went out at night,
moving through streets
too narrow for traffic.
The future was quoted
on posters by old men
always driven
in black sedans.
We walked past hotels
where clocks stood
silent in the rooms,
past women in green stockings,
war paint running
down their faces.
I remember, one night,
I said to no one:
*Tonight my heart's so heavy*
*that its gravity traps light*
*so people can only see us*
*as black ink*
*on this page.*
One of the women winked,
tattooed skull darkening
on her left eyelid.

## Way To Go

Some had drowned
In purple rivers of wine.
Others died bankrupt,
their hearts glued
to credit cards, cut to pieces
on expiration day.
Some died
with their eyes wide open.
Unable to sleep,
they started counting
onion shaped domes
jumping over
their ever present
Kremlin Wall.
Some died young,
killed by a foreign virus
as they got off
in the wrong part of town.
Earlier, all of them
had hitched a ride
with solitude speeding
through their daydreaming
in its black sedan.

## The Music Lesson

Naked, she rises and falls
and rises in the silver
waters of my mirror.
She laughs and says
my manhood is leaning
like the tower of Pisa
and she would let
my fingers do the walking
over the dark print
between her thighs.
The mirror sings
its reflection out
and the rhythm of images
is so vibrant, so strong
that I can't tell
where the glass ends
and music begins.

## Let The Good Times Roll

Our bodies moving light
years away from each other
on the glass
ceiling of her room.
She mimics women I have known:
Janet who ate dollar bills
when she was ten,
Monique whose eyes mimed
two broken stars
every time she dreamed
rivers of oil gushing
from the well
hidden part of her heart,
Giselle who wept
tiny bottles of vodka
wrapped in shreds of Pravda.
*Let the good times roll,* she says
and gold plated watches
come tumbling
from the pink void
between her thighs.

## Children's Park

They shoot
white suburbia
into their veins and
parents with no time,
Swiss bank accounts,
newspapers with their headlines
of junk bonds, murder, rape
electric chairs and
evenings with the sun
falling from the sky.
Their guardian angels
burnt to ashes,
gunned down
by god fearing clerics
goose stepping
through the bible.
They get stoned
on a new millennium,
all these children,
dying in the park.

## Through The Glass, Darkly

I tell her there's no turning back
and with a piece of glass,
vaguely outlining a sickle
or a broken hammer,
I cut her throat
and then mine.
We flow whichever way,
corroding everything in our path
and passersby take off their hats
thinking it's the right thing to do
with all that broken glass
and red rust at their feet,
with that dark river
rolling on and on
and earth turning slower,
at times almost grinding to a stop,
tilting slightly
with its vast seas of blood.

# My Lamp

leans towards the past,
its light attracting
ghosts of women
glimpsed in second rate
movies of my life.
Doreen, standing taller
than a fire station ladder,
Rosalie, covered with bracelets
flashing louder
than an upgraded semaphore,
Cynthia, blazing whiteness
and bitterness just like snow
drifting across steam grates
in the heart of Jesus
Saves neighborhoods.
When night falls,
we go on walking
searching for
the brightness
we left behind.

## Ma Bell

One day, the river
rose from its bed
and went walking
through my poems.
I followed behind and came
to the junction of many dreams,
didn't know which way to turn.
I thought then,
if only I could go sailing
from telephone pole
to telephone pole,
I would reach out
and touch the world.

## The Season Of Changes

Heat wave moved into town
and I watched Maureen
go up in smoke,
Kathy flicker as she fell
in ashes to the ground,
Elvira run like lava
down the slope of receding days.
I watched my poems
turn yellow, pages
letting go their words
and fifteen years
fading into stanzas
no one would read.

# IV Mr. Bureaucracy, Sister Alienation

## The Passport

When my father spoke French
with his heavy Russian accent,
syllables rolled off his tongue echoing
explosions rocking the outskirts of Kiev
in the winter of '17
when at the beginning of each day
the sun slowly rose,
a clenched fist.
I remember my father's smile stretching
across the passport's faded pages,
the top part of his head
buried by official stamps that said
no entry, no future, no exit, no past.

# Eclipse

At 2 P.M. the moon stepped
into the sun's path
and the eclipse was on.
The sky became
almost as dark as
uncle Igor's eyes
after his twenty five years
at digital life store.
Uncle Igor walking through
the glitter of business making,
the light in his eyes fading more
and more each day he crossed
the path of corporate ways.

## Sister Alienation

Did you ever cross the city,
your shadow so dark,
passersby thought they saw
the doorways of night roll?
Did you ever step
inside a post office
with the bird of revolution
singing on your shoulder
so letters written by lovers
flew through open windows
and circled for years
the county airport?
Did you ever lie down
on the pavement of a busy street
and the street became a desert
and the asphalt your pillow?

# Bad Neighborhood

Alienation came,
purple skirt slit
clear up to her waist. Evenings
she would walk the streets
and the sun looked on,
blood running down
its tired face.
Mr. Bureaucracy complained
about that uppity slut
being too good
for regulations,
too good
to pay taxes.
Every time I laid
my head on my pillow
the TV tower pushed
the sky away
from my window.
Late at night
the sandman would come,
walk softly across
the kitchen floor,
razor blades
jingling in his bag.

## Mr. Bureaucracy Moved In

and although the weather bureau
had predicted a dry day,
$$$ fell for 24 hrs
across the dreaming of the poor.
It rained so hard,
the sky lost all its money
and afterlife stocks fell so low,
Bureaucracy said he would
keep track of pennies deposited
on the eyes of the dead
although that money wasn't
working money anymore.

# Nocturnal Citizenship

At night, the TV tower is peaceful,
listening to dreamy clouds hum
old fashioned tunes of broken
love and sherry wine.
Rage comes with the morning sun.
All day, the tower screams
how lucky we are to live
where the sun gives away
so much gold every day.
Mirages invade the city,
evening sees the whole sky
burning. I close my eyes and
lower my head like a liar,
longing for night to fall.

## What The Gypsy Told Me

Those who recognize light
for what it really is,
an endless garden where
music lives its second life,
they will hear night sing
departure to every dawn.
Those who see stars as footnotes
penciled on the blank
spaces of dawn will later
sit in ice cream parlors
surprised by the flame of children
stories on their lips.
He who steals flames
from the tomb of the unknown
soldier to set fire to the Pentagon,
will go to bed with alienation
and his eyelids will be
butterflies soaring over
a desolate landscape of poems,
the ink of their verses
burning everything to ashes,
a dark flame of war rising over
the white silence of the page.

# Painting Time

The official colors,
they were all wrong.
Sun dials flattened themselves
into zeros, sort of miming
hard to read stamps,
the kind fading
at the bottom of shady
and hard to read
immigration papers.
The future was there,
an alien with no passport,
no past history,
no known address.
So, Mr. Bureaucracy
pushed hard to make red
the official color of time.
This way, he said,
every passing day
would be arrested
for reckless driving,
every hour, every minute,
every second would be guilty
and would be fined
for failure to come
to a full stop
in time.

## They Scream *Jordan*

*is USA river,*
selling salvation
between Western Auto
and Mike's bar.
There's no Jordan
on Main Street,
only a river of pick-up trucks
and beaten Chevrolets.
At night, it's a river of fire
rolling on and on
past x-rated movies, pawnshops
drug stores and hot dog stands.
All night I sit, drinking
vodka in Mike's bar,
waiting for Dostoevsky
to rise with the heavy smoke,
to come alive
in the voices of the room.
The woman next to me says,
*It's war out there.*
At dawn I return
to sleep all day,
to dream Jordan.
Over my roof,
the whole sky is burning.

# The Priest Next Door

Poverty smiles,
her language is not pretty
when she stumbles
through the census bureau,
messing up the GNP.
Her face is cracked
like the shell of an egg hatched
by some tropical bird,
lost in a winter of Manhattan.
She talks to herself...
There are numbers,
lots of numbers when she talks,
so many that
if you piled them up, surely
they would blot out the moon,
blot out the sun,
darkness would fall
for miles around.
The priest next door,
I see him go
through narrow alleys.
He moves as if
all of a sudden
he was walking blind.

# V River Café

## It's Not Easy

Writing poems about aging
facing blank pages at the River Café.
I write *time flows differently inside a poem*
and the page catches my reflection.
On the other side of the poem,
my father sits at his desk.
He jots down a new stanza,
a rose blooms on the tip of his pen.
He looks up, his face
younger than mine.

## Color Blue

During her sickness
my mother lost
her sunglasses.
The hospital room
became whiter and clocks
started to run slower.
Cars glided like swans
in black parking lots.
Later, I remembered
the color of her eyes.
It rained all day
so even at noon
the sun wasn't brighter
than a 40 watt bulb
blinking then dying
on the low
ceiling of the sky.

## Later In Life

I started to count days.
Numbers mocked me as if
I was adding books and rivers.
I couldn't understand
how years were multiplied
by so many losses.
When I reread my poems,
letters fell from their pages and
the remaining whiteness was
my own reflection.
I headed home and memories
turned streets to lava.
I then knew I was
many strangers.

## Clockwork Winding Down

When rain fell, I tried
to change water into letters.
Rain didn't want to write
poems anymore,
it curled around my fingers
and when night fell,
Dostoevsky wouldn't come
down Mike bar's flashing lights.
Neon remained unfocused,
a sick child
happy to make doughnuts
and car repair signs.
Dust went on strike refusing to rise
with the passage of each car,
refusing to be
specks of diamonds in the sun.
Often I forgot to greet
the newness of mornings
ascending over Earth
still talking in its sleep,
mornings brighter than
explosions of flowers,
melting down walls
as if they were wax.

# Disease

When I washed my hands
water didn't want to flow
around my fingers,
instead it drew
handcuffs around my wrists.
The doctor said my body
was like a gramophone.
He scraped my arm
with a long needle
and adjusted his stethoscope
to listen to the music
playing in my heart,
my heart humming a tune
no one else knew, a song
in the far away
whiteness of my bones.
Later when I was leaving,
the receptionist pressed
a dime against my lips
and I stood there,
weeping foreign stamps
on the worn carpet,
hoping to cry enough stamps
to send the whole office
many light years away.

## Once Upon A Time

I dreamed if I went sailing
from telephone pole
to telephone pole,
I would reach out
and touch the world.
I imagine what it would be like
to sail to the pole
that claims to be
the only orphan born
from father smoke
and mother mirror,
to the pole that has
a winter moon for face,
to the pole of the roaming unicorn
that neighs its sadness
at the steps of the power Co.
I dial the sun and say
*put poetry on the line*
and nostalgia comes running,
chasing images across
imprecise margins, barbwire
circling bygone years.
When I sleep I rise,
a one-winged angel,
long pillow pressed
tight against my back.

## When I Sleep

My bed rocks gently, a raft drifting
on the winding river of time.
Eyes closed, I ask the river why
clocks spoke Russian all day.
Rain in my sleep traces poems,
stanzas running Cyrillic
across slanted roofs
and streets leading to dead ends.
It writes what was
and could have been.
Rain keeps dreaming and
the blinding glare of water
changes everything so
the past and the future
shake hands halfway in time.
When I wake, my bed drifts
through curtained windows
and the door which strives
so hard to remain open
to voices of intelligentsia
asks why time always flows
so strange in the morning.

## The Visitor

When he drove into town,
the plaza clock turned
its face away, a shy bride
and just to please him
downtown windows took on
the look of chessboards
where black was winning.
Years went up in smoke,
nicotine stains on his lips
and I remembered
the many roads I walked,
running circles, not knowing
where my steps went.
Traffic lights spoke
their limited language of colors
red, the world stands still
green, that's resurrection time
arrows flashing left and right,
love is not a one way street.
From the steps of my porch
I watched the truck
that death rode
ignite the whole sky orange,
long after the sun had set.
The wind kept gently calling
names of places, names of friends
gone and lost
in that orange light.

## Regrets

When I came to the end of the road
I could have wept
all of Russia's onion-shaped domes
and my disappointments would have been
gas-lamps on strike against time.
I could have bled
nations of ink blots
migrating without passports
to discarded stanzas about trains
and my hesitations would have been
the birth of rhythm
in the customs office.
I could have wished small wings
on the tips of my eyelids
so I would be daydreaming
birds all day long
and nostalgia would be
the name of the land
where winged eyelids soar.
Late at night clocks speak
Russian in my room.
Clocks, they so often
speak of trains rolling
past their destinations,
all wrapped in smoke
and dreams, still looking
for that better world.

## At The River Café

I tell the driver that even
an emperor of clocks knows
his subjects tick
their own limitations,
and although clocks
often stood by my bed
spitting ashes on my poems,
they could never erase
my father's smile stretching
across his passport's faded pages.
The man nods, smiles
and says he understands.

# VI Riding The Subway

## Reasons

He went in no direction at all
because bright objects
were failing to reflect
the true meaning of his verse
and tomatoes, sold near water towers
refused to rent their redness
to the shame of revolutions
sold cheaper by the dozen.
He lost his way because words
couldn't pretend anymore
to be wedding rings
around his fingers
and he never understood that clocks,
in the final analysis,
weren't made to predict
the erratic path of disasters.

## You're Gone

And the sadness of dust
is no more confusing
than a beach ball dropped
down bottomless years
bouncing across sands
of summers long gone.
No more confusing than clouds,
gray priests drifting over
the skies of your hometown.
You're gone and palms
crowd parking lots,
demented immigrants
whose dreaming runs
swifter than the desert wind,
immigrants waiting for mirages
to come marching home.
You're gone and airplanes
jot down their sorrow
on the white haze
hanging this morning
over every airport.

## Coming Home

He left rainy roads, walked away
from armies of umbrellas on parade
with their amnesia of Cherbourg.
Left water towers, giving them
visions of what they could be,
spaceships softlanding
on uncharted poems.
Left armies of clocks
at the steps of the courthouse,
demanding a speed limit be put
on the passage of time
and asking no leniency be given
to dials harboring
24 hours revolutions.
Dark suited poets turn away
from sunny cafés
searching for his footsteps
in the dust of stars and icons,
now one foot high
in his favorite streets.

# Long Distance

At first we all went horizontal.
It was as if New York had fallen
flat on its face. Later,
tombstones started to click years
like odometers of runaway cars.
Pine boxes became telephone booths
from which we called collect
friends and relatives still alive.
After each call,
my neighbor's widow wept guilt
and wilted flowers on the ground.
She would stand very still,
her precious time slowly fading
into memories of clocks.

## Conversations

They were standing in my room.
I wrapped myself
around the suitcase
that had been mine
for many years
and was now picking up dust,
sadness still packed inside.
I wanted to write a poem
so I dreamed ink running down
the window's frost- covered glass.
One of them said:
*Look outside,*
*this was his kind of night,*
*dark rivers of absence flowing*
*over pale pages of ice.*

# Intersection II

My father jots down another stanza.
I ask him what the poem is about.
He looks up and spits
stars into the sky.
I then remember
him being gone
for many years
and surprised I fall
through the pages of my draft,
speeding past wars,
money and depression,
past Russian icons,
rivers and exiles,
past shattered mirrors,
music and lamp lights,
passing though
the orange pages
of my father's passport,
his smile, for an instant,
flashing a white diamond,
traffic sign screaming
slow down son
uneven images
straight ahead!

# Jim And I

We row the boat ashore.
Rain wrinkles
the surface of the lake and
all of a sudden I remember
the day clocks spoke
Russian in my room.
Sky and water intersect
as if sky was dreaming water
and water was painting sky.
Jim stands up and says:
*This is the sea of justice.*
*At night you come walking*
*to the edge of light and salt.*
*You talk in beehive rhythm*
*mumbling broken sentences*
*about the hours of the dead.*
At dawn dust rises,
draws question marks
over uncertain skies.
The eastern wind picks up,
my body, smoke rising
in that morning light.

## End Of A Republic

At first, clocks forgot
why they stood by my bed.
They became happy
instead of sad
and quit spitting ashes
all over my poems.
Shooting star bounced
off Napoleon's hat,
high into the sky,
and he lived
through many more poems.
Near the Russian church,
icons floated up
from Parisian cobblestones
right into my father's eyes
and the great republic of clocks
went broke, since time
wasn't money anymore.

## Memory

When the car radio played
one of his favorite songs,
Elvira started to run like lava
down the slope of receding days
and women in green stockings,
war paint running down their faces,
drifted with the music, thirty feet
over the highway line.
They rocked in the wind,
larger than life, dwarfing
every freeway sign.
A harsh wind
left its mark on their faces,
a foreign accent
on their parched lips.
The wind made them homeless
in the land of pretty images
and flowery love.

## There Came A Time

Tomatoes refused to be thrown
at poets signing
iambic peace petitions
and Dostoevsky grew four wings
then went walking,
a blue neon sign flowing counter
to Mike bar's flashing lights.
Dust started to sing again
its song rising,
an explosion of laughter
and diamonds in the blinding light.
Coming out of the subway
I suddenly felt
the heartbeats of the sun
against the wet pavement
and rain curling gently
poems around my fingers.

**André de Korvin** was born in Berlin, Germany from Russian parents. Raised in Paris, France. He has a Ph.D. in Mathematics from UCLA and has taught for many years at the University of Houston-Downtown. His first book of poems *The Four Hard Edges Of War* came out in 1992. A bilingual edition of that book (English and Italian) came out in 1999. *The Four Hard Edges of War* was later put into music (see third option). His second book *Dreaming Indigo Time* came out in January 2005. He was featured poet in 1989 at the Houston Poetry Fest and guest poet in 1998. He has been published in a number of literary magazines including *Buffalo Press, The Bayou Review, Bayousphere, IE., Arrowsmith, Green Fuse, International Voices, The Forum, Suddenly IV, The Texas Review, Lyric, The Weight of Addition* and *Time Slice* (two anthologies of Texas poets).

www.ingramcontent.com/pod-product-compliance
Lightning Source LLC
Chambersburg PA
CBHW060406050426
42449CB00009B/1916